THE SIX MIRACLES OF CALVARY

Discovery House Publishers

Books, music, and videos that feed the soul with the Word of God

Box 3566 Grand Rapids, MI 49501

WILLIAM R. NICHOLSON

THE SIX MIRACLES OF CALVARY
Unveiling the Story of the Resurrection

UPDATED IN TODAY'S LANGUAGE
BY DAN SCHAEFFER

The Six Miracles of Calvary
by William R. Nicholson
Copyright © 2001 by Discovery House Publishers

Discovery House Publishers is affiliated with
RBC Ministries, Grand Rapids Michigan 49512.

Discovery house books are distributed to the trade exclusively by Barbour Publishing, Inc.,
Uhrichsville, Ohio 44683.

Cover design by Vantage Group, Grand Rapids, Michigan.

Unless otherwise stated, all Scripture quotations are from the
Holy Bible: New International Version (NIV).

Library of Congress Cataloging-in-Publication Data

Nicholson, Wm. R. (William Rufus), 1822-1901.
    The six miracles of Calvary : unveiling the story
of the Resurrection / William R. Nicholson ; edited by
Dan Schaeffer.
        p. cm.
    Originally published: Chicago : Moody Press,
1927.
    ISBN 1-57293-072-1
    1. Jesus Christ--Crucifixion. 2. Atonement. 3.
Miracles. I. Schaeffer, Daniel, 1958- II. Title.

BT453 .N53 2001
232'.96'3--dc21   2001047285

Printed in the United States of America.

02 03 04 05 06 07 / CHG / 7 6 5 4 3 2

TABLE OF CONTENTS

✝

FOREWORD

I CONSIDER IT A WONDERFUL PRIVILEGE TO HAVE
been given the opportunity to reflect upon
and update William R. Nicholson's classic
book, *The Six Miracles of Calvary*. This book
contains magnificent insight into the meaning behind the six miracles that occurred that
day. The depth of Nicholson's spiritual
understanding of these miracles seems so rare
in our day and age, yet these miracles were
the very trumpets that God used to herald
the glorious message of the Resurrection.
Nicholson clearly reveals the purpose
behind each supernatural event and the confidence we may draw from them for our own
resurrection.

Each year, we seek to reproduce the "glory of
the Resurrection" in churches across the nation,
in both the simplest and most extravagant pro-
ductions, with music, singing, and drama. Yet
no staged glory can compare with the grandeur

that the true story of the Resurrection delivers to the human heart that will open to receive it. In these pages you will find the purpose behind the suffering of our Savior and the meaning behind the supernatural wonders of heaven at the moment of His precious death. And you will find the glory of Easter born anew in your heart.

God bless,
Dan Schaeffer, editor

1

THE MIRACULOUS DARKNESS

It was now about the sixth hour, and darkness came over the whole land until the ninth hour, for the sun stopped shining. (Luke 23:44–45 NIV)

THE MID-DAY DARKNESS IS THE FIRST OF THE SIX miracles of Calvary. It is the beginning of the divine procession of signs that heralded the death of Jesus Christ. Second came the supernatural tearing of the curtain of the temple. The third miracle was the earthquake and the splitting of the rocks, while the fourth miracle was the opening of the graves. The fifth miraculous sign was the condition of the empty tomb, and the last miracle was the resurrection of many saints who had died.

These were the six miracles of Calvary, all of them linked directly to the death of Jesus Christ. Some of these miracles occurred in the heavens, others under the earth, yet they all established a unique class of miracles. Each of these signs attached themselves irrevocably to Christ's eternal act of redemption. Each miracle, in its own special way, elucidates the meaning and purpose of the depths of our Savior's suffering. Together, all six surround Christ in His death, guarding carefully the truth of our deliverance through His blood.

The Scene Described

By the time the darkness descended, Jesus had already hung on the cross for three hours, from nine o'clock to twelve noon. Luke tells us that at noon, the "sixth hour," darkness blanketed the land.

This darkness was of a very special kind. First, it was "over all the whole land," or as Matthew states, "over all the land" (Matthew 27:45). No one can say for sure whether this extraordinary darkness covered half the earth, as darkness would normally do in the absence of the sun. But if this phenomenon was limited only to Judea, it was more amazing still, for it would then be an example of the kind of concentrated darkness that God sent upon Egypt for three days. In that case, only Goshen, where the Israelites lived, had light (Exodus 10:21–22). In any event, we know with certainty that darkness extended over the whole of Judea.

But this was a supernatural darkness. It was not the kind of darkness that preceded the earthquake that occurred at Naples in A.D. 79 when Mount Vesuvius became a volcano. That was a natural phenomenon in which smoke and ashes shrouded the sun's light from the earth below.

But this darkness extended far beyond the mount of Calvary, where the earthquake originated which was to follow it.

Not an Eclipse

It may be tempting to believe that an eclipse of the sun coincidentally occurred at the time of Jesus' crucifixion. The difficulty with that is that this darkness continued unabated for three hours. This removes any possibility of a solar eclipse, since the longest eclipse of the sun lasts only for a few brief minutes. Moreover, this darkness occurred during the festival of the Passover, which was always celebrated during the time of the full moon, when an eclipse of the sun is impossible.

And yet, in some inexplicable way, the sun was darkened. This was no normal eclipse. The light, in some supernatural way, simply failed. Nor was the darkness caused by the natural rotation of the earth shielding the sun's rays from half the planet, which causes night. It was dark at noontime, when the sun was at its zenith. This was a supernatural phenomenon, because darkness recoils at the first rays of sunlight. Yet here, the reverse occurred.

In nature, darkness, being the opposite of light, always succumbs to the more powerful rays of light. But here, the darkness at Calvary was so intense that it smothered the light. This is an amazing thing to consider. What a tremendous testimony to the almighty power of our God!

Did the darkness occur gradually, as the light slowly faded away, or did it come more suddenly? From Luke's words, "darkness came over the whole land until the ninth hour, for the sun stopped shining," we can conclude that the darkness began abruptly and ended abruptly at the end of the three hours. Suddenly the natural light failed, and three hours later, just as suddenly, the light returned.

Yet that is not to say that the darkness did not grow gradually deeper as the Savior's suffering on the cross grew ever deeper. The darkness is connected to the suffering of the Messiah on the cross. This seems to be corroborated by the cry of Christ at the close of these three hours. His silent perseverance ended at the conclusion of these three hours, as His sufferings had reached a climax and the darkness was banished.

Exactly how deep or black was this darkness? We are not specifically told, and yet, there is enough said to indicate that this was not simply a twilight fading of the sun, but an all-encompassing, frighteningly sudden and abysmal darkness.

The Three Hours

Up until the very moment the darkness began, what a busy three hours had passed on Golgotha! Our suffering Lord was busy, if we may use that term to describe His activity. He was deeply involved in the events swirling about Him. In those hours He spoke words of forgiveness to His crucifiers, and listened to the cry of the thief on the cross, granting him the assurance that this very day he would join Him in paradise. At the same time He recognized His mother, and assigned John to be the executor of His last will and testament concerning her care.

The soldiers were also busy watching Him, mocking Him, dividing up His clothes among them, and gambling for the seamless cloth. All the while the chief priests were busy criticizing Pilate's inscription on the cross, and venting their anger and indignation at Jesus. The priests, rulers, and crowd passed by Him in a wicked parade, making fun of Jesus, throwing sarcastic statements at Him, ridiculing, challenging, and cursing Him. All the raging waves of sin surged unchecked against Him, pounding against Him furiously and continually.

The Somber Silence

But what happens at the sixth hour? Silence. Sudden and somber silence. The very narrative speaks the word "darkness" and then itself goes silent. The hours between twelve o'clock to three o'clock are a blank page in the story, and the reader feels the solemn silence of the event. The evil, cruel taunts, the sarcastic comments, all are hushed now.

When these three hours of darkness ended and the light returned, all was busy and noisy again. Jesus ends this time by speaking, and the crowds begin to move around again. But during those three hours, we see only darkness, and hear only the sounds of silence. The divine Sufferer is silent, as if beneath that horrible darkness some huge horror shadowed His own soul. And everything is quiet. The taunts and insults stop. The crowds are distracted by the darkness. The dripping of His blood is deafening.

The darkness is frightening, and as the crowds experience this supernatural darkness, they tremble at the mysterious connection of this event to the crucifixion of Jesus.

The gospel writers do not make this connection for us, recognizing it is totally unnecessary. The darkness speaks for itself. The little they do say is like a parenthesis between what came before, and what follows that one little word—*darkness*. The darkness itself casts a shadow of silence over the whole three hours, giving the reflective reader time to appreciate how awful this foreboding gloom was. This was a dark, three-hour, divine pregnant pause, designed to arrest our attention.

And as a final exclamation mark on this incredible scene, the gospel writers close the story of the crucifixion and its incredible wonders. They do so by sharing the response of those who had experienced all these things. We read that the centurion and those who were watching "were terrified" (Matthew 27:54), and "beat their breasts and went away" (Luke 23:48).

The Reliability of the Record

Now that we've read the text, can we rely upon its historical accuracy? Yes, because God inspired the historians who wrote these words. Furthermore, we can add to their testimony that of the non-Christian historians who have referred to it, especially Celsus, the famous opponent of Christianity in the third century. The ancient church father Tertullian, at the close of the second century, was bold enough to proclaim to his non-Christian adversaries, "At the moment of Christ's death, the light departed from the sun, and the land was darkened at noonday, which wonder is related in your own annals and is preserved in your archives to this day."

But we rest in what the gospel writers have shared. I, for one, need no further corroboration of their testimony. Darkness did cover the earth, and with a cultivated Christian imagination we can sense the oppressiveness that miracle must have produced, as though we ourselves were feeling it.

How Do We Explain the Mystery?

What kind of event was this sudden darkness? It was a miracle, a visible suspension of the natural order of the universe. So we can see God at work in that darkness, because He, the great First Cause, is the only One who can interfere with the natural order which He established. In this miracle, He stepped out of the shadow of natural causes and displayed Himself to us as a living, involved, personal God, standing separate from His creation with "darkness under His feet" (2 Samuel 22:10 KJV).

Yet, while this was happening, the beautiful harmony of natural order remained intact in every other way. There was no natural cause which could have produced this darkness. God's natural order became the background for this miracle of darkness. The miracle did not send shock waves through the natural order, disturbing everything else, because the author of all creation Himself determined that it would create no disharmony. Despite the seeming discordance in the natural order caused by the miracle, not one aspect of the vast symphony of creation was strained, and not a note in the tune of creation went flat.

It was God's specific purpose to draw attention to Himself and His actions by performing a miracle that was contrary to all the laws of nature, all the while upholding nature by His great power.

When we think about how exclusively the darkness was connected to the death of Christ, we are given the most decisive proof of divine design. He was putting Himself on display. Jesus, the Son of God, was dying, and God the Father was making an appearance. The darkness became the background to the cross. He was both authenticating and interpreting for us the death of His Son.

What It Teaches

This miracle teaches us several things.

1. *This miracle of darkness was God's confirmation of Jesus' character and mission.*

When Jesus told people that He came to save them from their sins, they were offended by Him. When He said, "I am the Son of God," (Matthew 27:43) they took up stones to stone Him. "Show us a sign from heaven" (Matthew 16:1), they demanded. Now, the very thing they had demanded had been given to them, but their rejection of His person and purpose made the sign a terrible one. The heavens did give a sign—in fact the very order of nature bowed in reverence before the crucified Sufferer on that place of a skull. Even the Roman centurion exclaimed, "Surely He was the Son of God! (Matthew 27:54).

2. *The miracle of darkness magnifies the awesome significance of the death of Jesus Christ.* There is no other reason that God would highlight the death of His Son in such a supernatural and impressive way. Jesus had claimed that the purpose of His imminent death was to save us from our sins. He claimed that purpose for it on the night before He suffered, and many times before. Pardon from God and peace with God, on which our eternal life hinged, could be secured for us only through His blood and by His death on the cross.

And if that is true, was there ever anything of greater significance than this event in history? What could you compare this moment with? The universe, time itself, and all earthly concerns pale in comparison with this one event.

Was Jesus Deceived?

Jesus had always claimed that His death would have great significance, and He emphasized that all the way to the cross. He knew what the purpose of the cross was. He would pay for our sins, and bear our griefs and sorrows. Jesus told us, "I have a baptism to undergo, and how distressed I am until it is completed!" (Luke 12:50). This was the primary motivation of His earthly life. And although there was a joy set before Him upon the completion of His suffering (Hebrews 12:2), and that joy gave Him strength to face and endure what was coming, the cross was His consuming passion. This consuming zeal for the cross was what marred His beauty to us. It plowed the furrows of trouble into His face, and made Him the "Man of sorrows and acquainted with grief" (Isaiah 53:3 NKJV).

Did Jesus make a mistake regarding the significance of His death? Was His consuming interest nothing more than fanatical self-deception? God the Father answered that question when He parted the thin veil that separates this earthly world from the spiritual world, and visited Calvary with sudden darkness. The darkness was God's announcement, "Look, the Lamb of God, who takes away the sin of the world" (John 1:29).

3. *The miracle of darkness symbolizes the inconceivable suffering of Jesus Christ in His death.*

The sudden darkness was God's miraculous testimony to what Jesus was both experiencing and accomplishing because of our sins. The darkness expressed the sufferings that He was placing upon His Son. It was God who placed our sins upon Jesus, and the same God cast darkness upon the land about the cross of His Son and upon the hearts of those who witnessed this event. What the darkness communicated was that Jesus was "stricken by God, smitten by Him, and afflicted" (Isaiah 53:4).

God the Father had to wound, bruise, discipline, and lash His own Son. Christ suffered not merely from the physical crucifixion, but from the judgment and separation from His Father and the anguish He experienced in that separation. The perspiration "like drops of blood" that he sweated in the Garden of Gethsemane was created by the pressure of His Father's hand long before the harsh touch of the soldiers had ever been laid upon His holy body. The three hours of deathly darkness He suffered on the cross at Calvary perfectly illustrated the heaviness of His Father's hand upon Him.

No Longer Endurable

It was appropriate then, that before the period of darkness had completely passed, when the Son could no longer bear the Father's judgment against sin in silence, that He, with a startling voice and a sense of total wretchedness, looked into heaven and cried "My God, my God, why have you forsaken me?" (Matthew 27:46).

Yet the Father was there in the darkness, though for the time being He had been forced to forsake His Son in order to satisfy His perfect righteousness. The abandonment Jesus experienced, the punishment He received as the Sin-bearer, was perfectly represented in the deep, dreadful, total, and sudden darkness.

Christ bearing our sins in His body was not a fanciful story. It was a dreadful and awful reality Jesus had to experience.

Hid from Human Eyes

The darkness shrouded our Lord, and at the moment when He suffered the most extreme agony, His suffering was hidden from all human eyes. The impenetrable secrecy of those last hours is what enables us to imagine and appreciate the inconceivable suffering He endured. In His previous hours of suffering, He had been exposed to view. But human eyes were never intended to see Him in His supreme anguish. There is no way we could ever do justice in describing that horrible time, so God hid it from us.

If Jesus' experience as the Sinbearer revealed itself on His face, as Isaiah seems to indicate in his fifty-third chapter, and if it affected His appearance that men should take no notice of Him, then those last hours in which His sufferings climaxed must have impressed themselves on Him in unequaled severity.

Gethsemane is described for us in Scripture, but we read nothing about the last half of Calvary. Peter, James, and John were given an audience to His private suffering in Gethsemane, but at Calvary, God drew the drapes of darkness around Him to hide Him from human eyes.

Oh, the mysteries of that suffering! No man's eyes should ever see them. All that man was permitted to know of His suffering was to hear the terrible cry of incomprehensible pain and torment. Yet in that cry was the sound of certain victory, for the mournful cry, "Why have you forsaken me?" follows only upon the heels of the confident shout, "My God, my God."

What Does It Prove?

All the inconceivable sufferings of our Redeemer were symbolized by that terrible darkness. However, while the darkness was the symbol of the Father's righteous anger, it was also a proof of the Son's perfect righteousness. Only someone perfectly sinless, having no sins of His own to atone for, could be made responsible for sinners. So while He was indeed stricken of God, He was also the Beloved of God. He had indeed been appointed to suffer for our sins. But the depth of the suffering appointed to Him only mirrored the depth of the Father's delight and approval of Jesus' perfect life.

This serves to demonstrate the horrible evil and curse that is man's sin, since the only way to be saved is through infinite Love. At the same time we are shown that God's love is far stronger to save us than our sin is to destroy us.

Though the salvation Christ accomplished for us is glorious and brings us great joy, yet it was bought at great price. His birth foretold the grandeur of His coming work for us, and was appropriately announced by a shining light. But at His death, when the focus was on the staggering cost of that work for us, the light became darkness.

Redemption Accomplished

When the darkness was finally finished, because He Himself had passed through it, Christ was able to say; "It is finished!" (John 19:30). Redemption had been accomplished! Then, after crying aloud once more, but now in the voice of a conqueror so powerful that it split the rocks and opened the graves in anticipation of His own resurrection, He softly said, "Father, into your hands I commit my spirit" (Luke 23:46). In childlike trust and assurance He gave Himself into His Father's arms, surrendering His human life.

What It Pictures

The darkness of Calvary illustrated the doom of those who were crucifying Christ. It was the Father who had taken the Son's life in judgment, and the Son would have died even had the Jews not crucified Him. But for the same reason that it was just for God to judge Him in our place, since He is perfectly righteous, it was evil for them to crucify the Lord of Glory. "For they have persecuted him whom Thou Thyself hast smitten, And they tell of the pain of those whom Thou hast wounded" (Psalm 69:26 NASB).

Amos relates a remarkable prophecy concerning the future suffering of the Jewish people. "'In that day,' declares the Sovereign LORD, 'I will make the sun go down at noon and darken the earth in broad daylight'" (Amos 8:9). What an exact description of the scene on Calvary! Amos's prophecy relates to a future time of suffering for the Jews. But the darkness on Calvary was a sign, or a type, of that darkness to which Amos refers.

Concerning this prophecy, as Jesus was journeying toward His future crucifixion, He said, "For the time will come when you will say, 'Blessed are the barren women, the wombs that never bore and the breasts that never nursed!'" He added, "'They will say to the mountains, "Fall on us!" and to the hills, "Cover us!"' For if men do these things when the tree is green, what will happen when it is dry?" (Luke 23:29-31). In other words, if they do these things to Him, the green tree, the fruit-bearing vine of which His people were the branches, what shall God do to them, the dry tree?

By the momentous consequence of Christ's crucifixion, all those who reject Christ will be lost.

✝

Fellow brothers and sisters in Christ, the darkness of Calvary is gone, and the true Light is now shining. "The path of the righteous is like the first gleam of dawn, shining ever brighter till the full light of day" (Proverbs 4:18). On that future full day, the light shall never fail, and the days of our sorrow will be ended.

2

THE TEARING OF
THE CURTAIN

*At that moment the curtain of the temple was
torn in two from top to bottom. (Matthew 27:51)*

✝

IN THE PREVIOUS CHAPTER, WE EXAMINED THE MIRacle of darkness at noon, the first of the miracles of Calvary. The second miracle mentioned after the darkness is the tearing in two of the curtain in the temple.

Some people believe that it was the earthquake that caused the temple curtain to tear. If that were true, we would have to consider the earthquake as the second of the miracles sequentially. But it is rather implausible to believe that an earthquake that was powerful enough to cause the thick curtain of the temple to tear in two, did not also destroy the building in which it was hung.

What do the Scriptures tell us? "And when Jesus had cried out again in a loud voice, He gave up His spirit. At that moment the curtain of the temple was torn in two from top to bottom. The earth shook and the rocks split" (Matthew 27:50–51). If we follow the order here, the tearing of the curtain was independent of the earthquake. In fact, if we see here a cause and effect, it would seem that the tearing of the curtain was the result of the second of the two cries of Christ from His cross on Calvary, specifically, the last, loud, and final cry of the Crucified. That same cry would then also be responsible for the earthquake.

What Caused the Earthquake?

It seems clear that the tearing of the curtain in the temple and the earthquake were twin consequences of the same powerful cause, namely, the last expiring cry of Christ on the cross. That last loud cry of our dying Savior initiated both the tearing of the curtain of the temple and prompted the earthquake and splitting of the rocks.

This is suggested by Matthew's version of the account, and strengthened by Mark's. Although Mark mentions the tearing of the curtain and the last cry of the divine Sufferer, he fails to mention the earthquake. Matthew relates to us the impressions of the Roman centurion and guards who witnessed the crucifixion. They exclaimed, "Surely He was the Son of God!" (Matthew 27:54). Mark, who doesn't mention the earthquake at all, tells us that the centurion was powerfully moved by the final cry of Jesus on the cross (Mark 15:37–39).

When we compare the two gospel writers' accounts, it suggests that the incredible force of His cry on the cross is inextricably connected with the violent movement of the earth. Hence, if His cry is linked to the earthquake, it is also linked to the tearing of the curtain.

Therefore, in seeking to reconcile these two events, we have at the same time discovered a certain cause and effect relationship between them that is both solemn and inspiring. "With a loud cry, Jesus breathed His last," is immediately followed by, "The curtain of the temple was torn in two from top to bottom" (Mark 15:37-38). Dare we ignore the obvious association?

But now we must come to understand the nature of the curtain of the temple itself.

The permanent glorious temple succeeded the temporary and less glorious tabernacle, but the curtain of the temple was present in both. While there were many differences between the later temple and the earlier, portable, tabernacle, the curtain of the temple was simply a reproduction of the earlier version in both material and design. Regarding its purpose, it was identical.

Therefore, while the torn curtain was the one created for the temple, we must go back to the tabernacle to learn the purpose of the curtain in the first place.

The curtain of the temple was a covering designed to conceal what lay behind it, namely, the Holy of Holies, or the Most Holy Place.

Symbolism of the Tabernacle

The tabernacle had three divisions in it—the outer court, the Holy Place, and the Most Holy Place. Every Jew in Israel could assemble in the outer court. Only the priests were allowed to enter the Holy Place, where they would fulfill the daily tasks and ministries demanded of their positions. Yet the only one allowed to enter the Holy of Holies was the high priest, and he could enter it only once a year, with the blood of atonement and the smoke of incense.

In the outer court of the temple stood the bronze altar (Exodus 27:1–4) and bronze basin (Exodus 38:8). These were in the sight of the people and stood as symbols of what was needed to draw close to God. They reminded worshipers that they could not approach God without the ministry of the altar of blood sacrifice, and through that blood be cleansed as in a basin. Inside the Holy Place, in the sight of the priests who had just come from the bloody altar and the cleansing basin, were the bread of the Presence (Exodus 25:30), the golden lampstand (Exodus 25:31–40), and the golden altar of incense (Exodus 30:1–6)—symbols of union and fellowship with God.

In the Most Holy Place (Leviticus 16:2), only to be witnessed by the high priest, were the ark of the covenant (Exodus 37:1), its golden cover—the atonement seat (Exodus 25:17), the cherubim (Exodus 25:18–22), and the shekinah—the cloud of Glory. These were symbols of the throne of God's presence, power, and grace.

In this way, God communicated through the tabernacle's symbolism of sacrifice and cleansing the answer to how a sinner could worship Him acceptably.

The Meaning of the Curtains

Yet, the tabernacle also included symbols that represented the barriers to that same worship. During the ministry of the tabernacle, the approach to God was imperfect, for there were curtains in the tabernacle. Those in the outer court were blocked from the Holy Place by means of the first curtain; while the priests in the

Holy Place were blocked from the Most Holy Place by the second curtain. The purpose of each curtain was the same: it existed to conceal what lay behind it and to prevent any further passage beyond its boundaries.

By virtue of the bronze altar and cleansing basin, those in the outer court might enter to a certain point, but only the priests might pass the first curtain and come near to the symbols of fellowship with God. Only the one High Priest could go behind the second curtain and come near the even greater symbols of fellowship with God.

Of the two curtains, symbolizing barriers to entering into the presence of God, the second curtain was the more significant. For behind that curtain was symbolized within the Most Holy Place the culmination of the reality and blessedness of intimate communion with God. So ultimately, the Most Holy Place was where all the symbolism and ritual of temple worship, from the entrance in the gates of the outer court, to the entrance of the High Priest into the Most Holy Place, was directed.

This second curtain, which powerfully expressed the barrier to worship with God and which concealed the glory of God's very presence, is the one referred to here in our text.

The Second Curtain Described

The curtain was made of a curiously designed fabric. Upon the base of "finely twisted linen" (Exodus 26:31) were displayed the colors of blue, purple, and crimson. With the purple between the blue and crimson, beautiful cherubim were created in the pattern. Its visual effect prompted thoughts of life and power, while at the same time exhibiting both beauty and glory. It hung by hooks of gold suspended from four overlaid gold pillars. The Bible calls it the work of "skilled craftsmen" (Exodus 26:31). Yet it was the skill of God, who showed them the example from "the pattern I will show you" (Exodus 25:9). It was copied from "the pattern the Lord had shown Moses" (Number 8:4).

How impressive this sight must have been in the glow of the seven lights of the golden lampstand! How it must have filled the viewer with awe as it hung before them, concealing the greater glory which lay behind it. Through the picture of the embroidered cherubim, powerfully watching and guarding quietly, communicating clearly, "You may go this far, but no further." We can imagine the reverent whisperings of the priests in the Holy Place.

But now the curtain had gone out of existence. It had been torn in half. Suddenly and dramatically, its purpose is ended. While it still hung in place, you could now see through and beyond it. As a curtain it was useless. All at once, strangely, the concealment has ceased.

It wasn't as if the temple itself had been destroyed, or as if someone had simply vandalized it. Rather, it had simply become internally exhausted.

Resigning Its Office

The curtain fell in pieces in its own place before the Holy of Holies, as if it had resigned its office. No human act had caused its demise, nor had anything else from the porch of the temple to the Most Holy Place been moved or damaged throughout the entire magnificent building.

It was not through the natural process of decay that the threads of the curtain tore, because it fell not in shreds but into two whole pieces. It did not have a tear here and a gash there. It was torn in two, in *precisely* two pieces. As another gospel writer says, it was torn "in two" (Luke 23:45)—that is, in two equal pieces; thus its opening revealed the very center of what it had been created to conceal.

It was torn from the top to the bottom—in a straight line downward and completely through. It was not ripped apart from some vandal below, but cleanly cut by an invisible hand from above. This statement clearly implies supernatural intervention, indicating that anyone who saw it would recognize it as such.

But what is even more remarkable was that the tearing of the curtain was an amazing coincidence. When did the tear occur? It occurred precisely when Jesus Christ died on the cross— at the very moment! That was the precise moment the curtain of concealment had been waiting for; the moment for which through all the ages it had continued to exist in defiance of the ravages of time and violence. The very moment! It was as though an inner intelligent clock had kept watch within it and when it heard the final stroke, the final cry of Christ, it knew its time and purpose had come to an end.

Cry of Victory

It is noteworthy to remember that it was torn immediately after the loud cry of the crucified Christ. There were, in actuality, two loud cries from the cross. The first came just before the darkness had ended; the second came after the darkness had passed. The first cry was an agonizing wail of abandonment; the second was a shout of joy. The first cry was crushed out of Him by an intolerable agony of which the dreaded darkness was a sign; the second cry was the thrusting forth of His feelings of fulfillment and deliverance in being restored to communion with His Father. The first cry shouted, "My God, My God, why have you forsaken Me?" (Matthew 27:46). The second cry was a shout that said nothing, but followed His last words, "It is finished" (John 19:30).

His work was finished. He had borne our sins. His burden was gone. So this second loud cry from the cross was the Conqueror's roar of victory. In the same way that a weary man at the end of a long day reflects pleasantly upon the success of the day, relaxing with gratifying visions for the next day, so with an intensely human joy, before falling asleep, the suffering Savior gave forth that final shout. His triumphal purpose was accomplished.

The proof of His victory was evidenced in the supernatural power of a dying man's voice. The Roman centurion was overwhelmed by it, and the earth itself shook in response to it.

That roar of victory coincided with the tearing of the curtain. As the Savior finished His work, as His note of triumph rose high and clear from His dying lips, then the concealment of the Holy of Holies came to an end. The curtain was cut as if by the blade of a skilled artisan, passing swiftly down the curtain, ending the concealment forever. It was a sign of what had been accomplished.

Here we find something so conspicuously divine that we must stop and ponder it. It had been accomplished so that we would think about it and learn from it. Not only does the Word of God record this divine moment and act, but the manner in which it was recorded draws our mind's eye to the picture. The manner in which it was accomplished suggests that there would inevitably be witnesses, and as a matter of fact, there *were* witnesses.

The specific time it occurred was one of its most compelling features. Jesus Christ died at three o'clock in the afternoon. This was precisely the time the evening sacrifice would begin, requiring the presence of the priests in the Holy Place, in front of this very curtain. They would be fully engaged in their priestly duties. Yes, God meant it to be seen and reflected upon.

Enemies Silenced by Proof

We need to pause here to note how strong the proof is in the gospels of the tearing of the curtain. The gospel writers were certainly bold enough to publish their accounts in the midst of the Jews and under the very eyes of the priests. Were they ever contradicted? How such a blatant contradiction would have been used by those ever watchful unbelievers Celsus, Porphyry, and Julian! But there was nothing they could say. They could not even claim that they had never heard of the event. The simple declaration of the evangelists proves itself. This is the true story of how the curtain was destroyed.

Truly God meant for us to learn from this powerful event. The effect it should have on us can be deduced from the sacredness of the veil that so completely controlled the conduct of the priests. For fifteen hundred years, as greatly as the people of God had sinned, there was one sin they had never committed—they had never violated the secrecy of the curtain. Therefore, when the curtain was torn in two, the impression upon those who witnessed it must have been strange and confusing. The impact upon the priests must have been tremendous, and the inevitable reports of this incredible event must have stirred the community with excitement.

Could the coincidence of the precise moment of the tearing of the curtain and the final death-shout of Christ have failed to turn reflective thinkers Christ-ward and cross-ward? To prove the powerful effect this event had upon the priesthood, one only needs to see that as soon as the gospel was preached, "a large number of *priests* became obedient to the faith" (Acts 6:7).

And forever the Scriptures will declare to us, "Behold," look carefully at this sight, this visual lesson from God, for in the tearing of the curtain we find the very gospel symbolized.

The way our dying Savior's victory was demonstrated in the tearing of the curtain reveals the consequences to the temple where it had hung. The changes that occurred were, by analogy, a result of the Crucified's victory.

What the Evidence Proves

First of all, because the curtain was now torn, it became virtually impossible for the high priest to continue to carry *inside the curtain* the blood of atonement.

Secondly, the fifteen-hundred-year secrecy of the Holy of Holies had come to an end, and all its deepest mysteries were now open to full view.

Third, the priests who once could only minister *in front* of the curtain were now free to enter safely into the very presence of God, previously symbolized by the Most Holy Place.

Lastly, the people in the outer court could also freely proceed into the Holy Place of the priests, and from there, like the priests themselves, into the Holy of Holies. For when the very place of God's holy presence had ceased to be concealed, the spirit and meaning of the first curtain was also concluded.

The tearing of the curtain, therefore, spelled doom for the tabernacle system. It removed the meaning from the very structure of typical temple worship. It severely altered the rituals and neutered the divine program for which they had been put into existence. And since it spelled the end of the divine dispensation of the temple sacrifices and offices, it also removed the wall that separated Jew and Gentile and threw open the Holy of Holies to all who would enter.

These were the spiritual results, but what about the real and practical results? How did it ever happen that a program of worship, so beset with concealment and barriers, was ever instituted by God? Why did He preclude men from His presence and order that none should approach Him except under the protection of sacrificial blood? The reason was sin. Sin was the obstacle, the obstruction. The arrangement of the temple, with its concealing curtains, was God's solemn assertion that He would not fellowship with a man whose sin was still upon him, unforgiven, its damning curse ingrained in his entire being.

So when the curtain, the sign of the separation sin had created between man and God was removed, it signified that the sin which had created the need for the curtain had also been removed. What had been symbolically accomplished in the tearing of the curtain had been practically accomplished in Jesus Christ. This was the victory behind His death. He who had never sinned had gone to war for us against our sin and conquered it. He, the innocent divine Sufferer, gave the required suffering for sin in His own person.

The Question of Sin Settled

And so, the High Priest was removed from his office by God Himself, through that shout of triumph from the cross that tore open the curtain. Now the Crucified Himself, the real High Priest, would carry His own blood, once for all, not into the symbolic presence of God but into His real presence in the heaven of heavens. There He dwells in the eternal power of an endless life, offering His own righteousness to any sinners who would place their faith in His blood and sacrifice for their sins.

In this way He has settled forever the problem and obstruction of the sin which barred man's intimate fellowship with God. No further obstructions remain for those who would draw near to Him through faith in Christ.

Man May Now Approach God

As a result, the way is now open for man to approach God. By faith, in spiritual worship, we have "confidence to enter the Most Holy Place by the blood of Jesus, by a new and living way opened for us through the curtain, that is, His body" (Hebrews 10:19–20).

In a way, the torn curtain exemplified the torn humanity of Christ when He died on the cross. In the fine linen of the curtain we can see typified the righteousness of His human nature. The hooks of gold that suspended the curtain represent His divine nature, the dependence of His humanity upon His deity. In the heavenly blue and earthly crimson, and the blending of the two together into the purple between them, we see heaven and earth blended together in His human life in a beautiful and rich tapestry. In the cherubim, which all the colors skillfully create together, we see the supernatural purpose of His life in human history.

Christ the Perfect Man

The humanity of Jesus was indeed the skillful work of God. Its design was so amazing that it was hidden from us, concealed behind a curtain of flesh. God displayed the perfect man in His Son, the only kind of man whom God would permit to approach Him. His perfection, if considered merely on its own, would have destroyed our hopes of approaching God. His becoming flesh would have been of little use to us without His sacrificial death on our behalf. The curtain of His flesh had to be torn.

His humanity was completely and thoroughly torn—torn "from the top." It was God who struck Him, tearing Him "to the bottom," causing Him to be sorrowful even unto death. He was torn so completely that through His perfect sacrifice, we sinners might come immediately into the presence of God. We can now look by faith directly into heaven. We can now look at Him with our faces unveiled, and though His glory is strong and powerful, gently His lovely glory descends upon us.

There is nothing hidden from us, no anger held in reserve for us, no blazing wrath of God for us, even though well deserved. The words "Abba Father" were never spoken to the Father by the lips of man until Jesus taught us to do so. But now the child of God can find his own way into His Father's loving embrace, and embrace Him back.

3

THE MIRACULOUS EARTHQUAKE

The earth shook and the rocks split.
(Matthew 27:51)

THIS THIRD OF THE CALVARY MIRACLES HAS A SIG-nificance as a link in a chain of wonders. For it was not only the cause of what followed—the opening of the graves—but was also a sign of great magnitude and power by itself. As with the darkness and the tearing of the curtain, this was a supernatural exclamation mark by which God communicated not only the importance of the death of Jesus Christ but also the true meaning behind it.

Get the Facts Straight

The first thing we need to do is get the facts straight. "And when Jesus had cried out again in a loud voice, He gave up His Spirit. At that moment the curtain of the temple was torn in two from top to bottom. The earth shook and the rocks split" (Matthew 27:50–51).

The earthquake occurred at the instant of Christ's final great shout of victory and His death. That death was His victory and the earthquake bore testimony to the power of that truth.

Strength of the Concussion

The testimony of the earthquake was not a small one. The strength of the quake was such that *the rocks were split*. Even if the splitting of the rocks had been minimal, it still would have been evidence of a powerful quake.

However, that is not the case. The rocks were not split in the sense that a small crack or fissure could now be seen in them. They were split apart with such power as to lay open and unobstructed the interior of rocky graves, of which there were many on Golgotha. This was no minor trembler. In proof we have only to return to the witnesses, the Roman soldiers who saw both the crucifixion and experienced the quake. Their response to these events is that they "were terrified" (Matthew 27:54).

The power of the earthquake was an appropriate and expressive response to the final shout of the Savior in victory; completely appropriate to the magnitude of the death to which it testified.

Extent of the Earthquake

Nothing definite is recorded about the extent of the earthquake. The word *earth* may mean no more than land, and it is quite possible that the quake was felt only in the regions of Judea. Furthermore, it is likely that it was the area surrounding Calvary that would probably have felt the greatest impact, since it was at that point that the cause for the disturbance originated. It was there, beneath the cross that testified to His victory, that the shifting earth would reverberate the hardest.

Proof of the Event

Whether certain non-believing historians of the past took notice of this earthquake is of no concern, for which of them were likely to have been present at Calvary? Even if they had been present, or had heard the report concerning it, how likely would they have been to recognize the Christ-like purpose which occasioned it, and thus set it aside for special mention among the world's noteworthy earthquakes?

It is sufficient that Matthew recorded it publicly and thereby challenged those who were witnesses to disprove it. Its obvious purpose and placement in the story harmonizes well with the other miracles. It would not, to quote another, "be right, altogether to reject the testimonies of travelers to the extraordinary tears and fissures in the rocks near the spot. Of course those who know no other proof of the historical truth of the event will not be likely to take this as one; but to us who are convinced of it, every such trace soberly and honestly ascertained, is full of interest."

The Nature of the Event

So far we have ascertained the facts. But now we may ask, "What sort of event are we to consider the earthquake to be?" We have called it supernatural and referred to it as miraculous, but aren't earthquakes frequent in nature? So why should we regard this particular earthquake as special or different from all the rest?

A supernatural event is an event caused by the direct intervention of God. But there are times when God directly intervenes within the established order of nature, for example, when in answer to prayer, He causes it to rain. Though the event is supernatural it is not miraculous. While God does specifically intervene at such a time, He uses the forces already at work in nature to accomplish His purpose.

In contrast, a miracle is something which, while it is the result of the direct intervention of

God, is not caused by the natural forces of nature. It is caused exclusively and instantaneously by an act of His will, such as when Jesus turned the water into wine.

Supernatural and Miraculous

We claim that this earthquake was not only supernatural, but unnatural as well, that is, it was miraculous. It was supernatural in the sense that it was the result of the direct intervention of God, but it was unnatural in that it was not a result of any of the natural causes of earthquakes. God interrupted the natural order of nature, and solely by an act of His will caused the earth to shake violently.

Four Coincidences

In proof of what was just said, consider the great coincidences surrounding the earthquake.

First, the earthquake coincided with the death of Jesus Christ. The writer of the gospel clearly implies that the earthquake was directly connected to His death, and would not have taken place otherwise.

Secondly, the earthquake occurred at the same time as the miraculous darkness and the tearing of the curtain. It was one of a cluster of miracles and can only rightly be considered in relationship to the other wonders.

Thirdly, the earthquake coincided perfectly with the Savior's shout of victory from the cross. It wasn't internal fires under the earth that caused the earth to shake, but a voice above the earth, the voice of redemption accomplished, the shout of the Laborer finally entering His rest.

The Cross Was Shaken

Fourthly, the earthquake coincided with the splitting of the rocks and the opening of the graves. Strangely, as violent as the earthquake was, it disturbed nothing else. It did not shake the Savior's cross down, though Calvary itself was trembling. While the earthquake opened graves, it did not open *all* the graves at Golgotha, only the graves of the saints.

It is almost as if the earthquake were a living thing whose divine intelligence was able to discriminate among the dead buried at Golgotha. It seemed to sense the meaning behind the shout of victory and applied every one of its violent movements intelligently and specifically to accomplish only that which would affirm the purpose of His death. It seemed to look forward to His resurrection victory on the third day. In this sense it summarized all the other miracles.

When all these coincidences are taken into account it seems plain that the earthquake at Calvary was not a result of natural causes. It seems rather that nature was preempted from its natural course through a supernatural act of God, designed to reinforce the meaning of Christ's death on the cross.

The Testimony of the Earthquake

And now we need to ask what the earthquake's particular testimony to the death of Jesus Christ was.

It is clear that it had a confirming purpose all of its own. Naturally it was used to open the graves, but that couldn't have been the sole reason for its occurrence. As we have seen, the victory shout from Jesus on the cross, which took place before the earthquake, was also essential to opening the graves. If the earthquake did not have a unique purpose all to itself, it was a wasted miracle, something inconsistent with the plans of God. The gospel writer leaves no such impression. On the contrary, the reader is compelled to think about how each of the miracles occurred in unique reaction to the death of Christ.

Calvary Answering Sinai

And what of those who experienced the earthquake? Did they quickly forget the earthquake as soon as the graves were opened? The answer is no. As a matter of fact, they could not have known at the time why the graves had opened, and only concluded that it was as a result of the earthquake. The earthquake, therefore, exerted a moral effect of its own upon them. It was a sign by itself.

What then is the appropriate testimony of the earthquake?

First, it was Calvary's answer to Sinai. Hundreds of years earlier there had been an earthquake on Sinai; now there was an earthquake on Calvary, and the wrath of the former was now being stilled by the mercy of the latter.

Why the Laws at Sinai?

It was upon Mount Sinai that God had dispensed His law. Of course, moral obligation and responsibility had existed before the giving of the law, but on Sinai God drafted our responsibility and duty before Him. His purpose in this was that His law could be remembered and referred to and might become holy to the people.

The law that God dispensed at Sinai revealed the utter sinfulness of man. While human sin had certainly existed before the giving of the law, the declaration of it at Sinai thrust it forth prominently before men and stripped it of all its disguises. The law made sin appear in its true light—entirely evil, a permanent blight upon the soul of man, without any trace of merit whatsoever.

The Meaning of the Terrors

In response to the horrors of sin, God revealed Himself as the awesome Guardian of truth and righteousness when He descended upon Mount Sinai. "There was thunder and lightning, with a thick cloud over the mountain, and a very loud trumpet blast. Everyone in the camp trembled. Then Moses led the people out of the camp to meet with God, and they stood at the foot of the mountain. Mount Sinai was covered with smoke, because the Lord descended on it in fire. The smoke billowed up from it like smoke from a furnace, the whole mountain trembled violently" (Exodus 19:16–18).

By creating a visual scene that would forever impress upon their hearts and minds His attitude toward sin, through the terror of what they saw, and what they heard, He was able to communicate the terrible evil effect of sin upon their soul and conscience.

In this way God communicated the horror of sin and His hatred and intent to destroy it. But their sin permanently stained their lives, making it impossible for them to free themselves from its grip. Sin renders man helpless and ruined. For, "Who can withstand His indignation? Who can endure His fierce anger? His wrath is poured out like fire; the rocks are shattered before Him" (Nahum 1:6).

A Prophesy of Grace

God enacted this terrifying scene to teach men about the horrible reality of sin. The terrors of Sinai were only a rehearsal; they were not to be the final infliction of punishment, they were intended as a warning and an instruction to the sinner, designed to create within him a desire to be saved from God's punishment of sin. The terrors displayed on Sinai were a prophecy that Christ, the Guardian of truth and righteousness, would insert Himself to do for us what we are helpless to do for ourselves.

In this sense, Sinai was the forerunner to Calvary. And so, "when the time had fully come, God sent His Son, born of a woman, born under law, to redeem those under law" (Galatians 4:4–5). Christ died for us. He endured the overwhelming weight of our sins and suffered those horrors of which the terrors of Sinai were but a picture.

Calvary Absorbed Sinai

Calvary quenched the fires of Sinai. It did so with a darkness so dark that the light could not appear, causing even the bravest of men's hearts to quail. It did so by the loud wail of His suffering that echoed throughout the darkened sky, whose depth of anguish only He could ever express. It became manifestly clear even to us that the scene at Calvary was the more powerful and awful of the two.

The Finished Work

But finally, the darkness passed and the sufferings ended. The great work was finally accomplished, making it possible for God to be both just and the Justifier of all who would believe in Jesus. The great terrors of Calvary, which had demoted the lesser ones of Sinai, were now themselves lost in the sweet mercies of Calvary. The shout of Calvary's victory was heard over the trumpet sound of Sinai's wrath.

Sinai was the prophecy of Calvary; Calvary was the fulfillment of Sinai. Sinai portrayed the sinner's wretchedness and destruction; Calvary, the sinner's recovery and blessedness. Sinai was God's firm voice of condemnation; Calvary, God's gentle, fatherly voice of pardon and peace.

Joy Instead of Pain

Because the earthquake had to bear witness to the teaching of Sinai first, it then had to bear witness to an equal reality in the teachings of Calvary. Whereas at Sinai the earth shook as if convulsed with pain, at Calvary the earth shook as if overcome with joy. It communicated clearly that Calvary's mercy is as powerful as Sinai's vengeance. One earthquake answered the other. And in the meantime, from the lessons of both, we are taught to say, "Love and faithfulness meet together; righteousness and peace kiss each other" (Psalm 85:10).

Creation's Share in the Victory

And yet the earthquake gave testimony a second time to Christ's death. It was the reaction of the physical creation to the work of redemption. Jesus Christ shouted His achievement at the culmination of His work, and "the earth shook." That was no coincidence. Creation had been effected by His victory, and it expressed itself. And why shouldn't the earth have been affected by what Christ accomplished on the cross?

Didn't man's sin bring a curse upon the earth? Thorns and thistles, floods and droughts, the sweat and tears of work, the savageness of wild animals, and all the myriad dangers found within nature are merely the footprints of man's sin. If, then, man's redemption is as real as his sin, why shouldn't the earth feel its effects?

It almost seems as if man and earth are one dynamic organism, the whole science of physical geography and geology being a systematic expression of the relationship between the two—of their continual action and reaction upon one another. Is it so unbelievable that such a fundamental change in man's condition, such as his redemption, could occur and creation not express it in some way?

Millennial Glory

When we remember that the scriptures tell us that one day the earth itself will be recreated—a physical regeneration which will complement the world's moral glory under the reign of Christ—we can't help but see in the earthquake of Calvary not only a promise, but a down payment upon the fulfillment of those prophesies.

We referred to the earthquake as the earth convulsing with joy. While that is figurative speech, it is not mere rhetoric. There is a substantial scriptural basis for the pictorial assertion. In Romans Paul speaks of "the whole creation . . . groaning as in the pains of childbirth right up to the present time" (Romans 8:22). Paul also says, "The creation waits in eager expectation for the sons of God to be revealed. For the creation was subjected to frustration, not by its own choice, but by the will of the one who subjected it, in hope that the creation itself will be liberated from its bondage to decay and brought into the glorious freedom of the children of God" (Romans 8:19–21).

Paul even goes so far as to attribute to the physical creation the feeling of *hope*. Here we have the authority of Paul for representing the convulsing of the earth with joy as a foretaste of the millennial glory it will one day taste when "all the trees of the field will clap their hands" (Isaiah 55:12). One day "the moon will shine like the sun, and the sunlight will be seven times brighter like the light of seven full days" (Isaiah 30:26).

> And sunshine, such as earth has never
> known
> Shall fill these skies with mirth,
> And smiles, and beauty
> Erasing each sad wrinkle from their brow,
> Which the long curse had deeply graven
> there.

Yes, in an earthquake of joy, a convulsion of delight, creation was anticipating its own regeneration; though at this time,

> The whole creation groans,
> And waits to hear that voice,
> That shall restore her comeliness,
> That shall make her wastes rejoice.
> Come, Lord, and wipe away

The curse, the sin, the stain,
And make this blighted world of ours
Thine own fair world again.
Come, then, Lord Jesus, come.

4

THE MIRACLE OF THE OPENED GRAVES

The tombs broke open. (Matthew 27:52)

+

THE FOURTH OF THE CALVARY MIRACLES WAS THE opening of the graves.

That disturbed graveyard has a distinct place among the Calvary miracles. In fact, it may be the most remarkable of all the miracles we have considered to this point. It is the climax of all the previous miracles, even as it anticipates the miracles that will follow.

First of all, let's consider the facts related to us in the gospel.

"When Jesus had cried out again in a loud voice, He gave up His spirit. At that moment the curtain of the temple was torn in two from top to bottom. The earth shook and the rocks split. The tombs broke open and the bodies of many holy people who had died were raised to life" (Matthew 27:50–52).

So we can clearly see that it was by means of the earthquake that the graves were opened. We may also conclude that most of the graves, if not all, were located at, or around, Calvary. As we mentioned earlier, the earthquake would likely have been the most violent at its point of origin—the epicenter of His disturbing death. It is certain that a graveyard existed near Calvary, since Jesus was laid nearby in Joseph's tomb.

Fixing the Locality

If, as we believe, this miracle was meant to be seen as a testimony to the power of Christ's death, it would necessitate the graves being in close proximity to the cross. Further indication that these graves were close to Jerusalem is seen from the fact that when the saints were resurrected, they immediately entered Jerusalem (Matthew 27:53). Where these resurrections took place is important.

It can also be reasonably implied that these particular graves were rocky tombs, holes carved into the rock whose entrances were sealed by large stones rolled in front of them. We can infer this because of the obvious connection between the two statements "the rocks split" and "the tombs broke open."

Distinction Between Force and Design

Since it appears that the opening of the graves is so closely connected to the splitting of the rocks, why separate these two events?

The reason they must be seen separately is because there is a significant distinction between the two events. The splitting of the rocks was evidence of *force*, while the opening of the graves was evidence of *design*. The splitting of the rocks did not, by itself, foretell anything to come. The opening of the graves, however, was like the first budding of the coming resurrection glory.

As we said before, the earthquake, as an event, was not simply the means to open the graves, but an independent miracle with its own distinct meaning. In the same way, the opening of the graves was not simply the logical result of the earthquake, but an event with its own unique meaning and importance. It is the fourth in this amazing sequence of Calvary miracles. It was the instantaneous result of the earthquake, in the same way that the earthquake was the instantaneous result of Christ's shout of victory from the cross. And like the earthquake, it occurred in response to that shout. The moment Christ died, the graves opened.

Whose Graves Were They?

Significantly, it was only the graves of saints, God's children, Christ's people, who were opened. Not one person's grave was opened whose soul did not have a saving interest in the death of Christ, to which the opening of the graves was the marvelous answer.

It is such a beautiful picture. All those graves of God's children, each and every one of them individually and lovingly selected, were to His eyes the most important places in the entire world!

It is instructive to note that while the graves were opened at the moment of Christ's death, the bodies did not arise from them till after His own resurrection—on the third day. "They came out of the tombs, and *after* Jesus' resurrection . . ." (Matthew 27:53, emphasis added). The record makes it plain that they were not raised until He was.

So for the moment we are not considering the resurrections themselves, but simply the opening of the graves. The opening of the graves had a significance beyond simply being necessary to release the resurrected from their tombs. The opening of the graves was not simply a physical necessity for the resurrections, any more than it was a mere physical consequence of the earthquake.

It was, in fact, a marvelous act of preparation that needed to be accomplished at the moment of Christ's death, and timed to occur at precisely the moment our Savior Himself entered among the dead. It could not be put off until He returned from the dead, although what He intended to accomplish among those who would be resurrected had to be delayed until then.

In view of all these circumstances, how powerfully does the miracle assert itself! We are overwhelmingly convinced that God's intervention here is one of the clearest and most powerful of His precious testimonies to the death of Jesus Christ.

Secondly, the sense that something precious is being revealed to us seems warranted by the clear facts of the matter. The fact that the graves were opened at the instant of Christ's death, but the resurrections did not take place until the third morning afterward, shows that the opened graves were intended to be an *exhibition*.

Meant for an Exhibition

If the sealed rock tombs were opened by the earthquake merely to permit the resurrected bodies to escape, then the earthquake should not have taken place until the moment of their resurrection. But the fact is that those graves were opened from Friday afternoon until Sunday morning and exposed to thousands of spectators. No attempts to seal them back up during the intervening Sabbath would have been permitted. Doesn't it seem clear, then, that the opening of the graves was intended to be an exhibition, that it had a story to tell?

What Kind of Resurrection?

Again we ask, why were the graves opened at all? What sort of resurrections were these? Were they examples of what the apostle calls the "better resurrection" (Hebrews 11:35), the final glorified resurrection body? Or were they, as in the case of Lazarus, merely the resurrection of their mortal, earthly bodies?

It can be proved through Scripture that they were the latter, as I shall try to show later in this chapter. The point to be made here, however, is that the opening of the graves implies an earthly resurrection, because the idea that the gravestones needed to be moved aside so that their spiritual resurrection bodies could be released is illogical. A spiritual body has spiritual properties. In His resurrection body, Jesus entered the room where the apostles were assembled without going through the door. It is His resurrection body, we are told, that is the true model for all resurrected saints.

Would this kind of a resurrection, therefore, be dependent on an open grave? No, in the same way that the departure of our human spirits from earth is not dependent upon breaking down the walls and ceiling of the room in which we die.

Christ's Resurrection Is Different

We see this truth demonstrated in the coming forth of Jesus' body from the grave. While it is true that the great stone that sealed His tomb had been rolled away, He had left the tomb before that event took place. The removal of the stone soon after His resurrection was to show the disciples that the tomb was empty, and therefore convincing them of His resurrection. An angel accomplished this removal of the stone, but at the moment it was performed, Christ was no longer there.

On the other hand, when Lazarus was raised, he was called back into his original body, and therefore the command was to "Take away the stone!" (John 11:39).

For these reasons it becomes clear that the opening of the graves at Calvary is consistent with only one conclusion, that what they experienced was only their natural earthly bodies being resurrected. They had not yet received their final glorified resurrection bodies.

Revived Not Risen

Those saints who were raised from their graves were not, by themselves, an adequate expression of the victory of Christ, in the sense that is expressed in 1 Corinthians chapter fifteen, for they were not yet *risen* from the dead, but only *revived* from the dead.

But it was such an amazing event that it nevertheless illustrated and affirmed the truth of the better, future resurrection. When Jesus said, "I am the resurrection and the life" (John 11:25), He then proceeded to revive the dead body of Lazarus to illustrate the truth of the resurrection, even though what Lazarus was experiencing was not the final and glorified resurrection.

Why a Limited Number?

This explains why only a limited number of graves were opened. This was not their final resurrection and God was not playing favorites by raising only a few chosen saints. All of God's children are dear to Him, but reviving just a few believers suited the purpose of what He was teaching them, and at the same time sufficiently called attention to the occasion. Enough graves were opened to provide an illustration of the power of the cross, and the power displayed by those open graves furnished an example for all God's people for all time.

And now, thirdly, what is really being taught here?

A symbol is a sign that represents an idea. For example, a lamb is the symbol of meekness, because a lamb does not resist, although the human meekness it symbolizes is of a superior quality. In the Old Testament a slain lamb was the symbol of Christ crucified, because its shed blood actually satisfied certain ceremonial offenses; although a ceremonial satisfaction was not as great as the real satisfaction of sins by Christ.

Symbol of the Glorious Resurrection

The opening of the graves symbolized the removal of all obstructions to the final glorious resurrection, because it removed the obstacles to raising the revived dead bodies of the saints. But sealed grave tombs, even when sealed with rock, are only flimsy obstacles compared with the difficulty involved in the final, glorious resurrection.

Consequently, it signified that the better resurrection was now in operation. Whatever had made it impossible for the corrupted physical bodies of the saints to be raised in incorruption, whatever had made such resurrection impossible, was now, by virtue of those opened graves, removed.

And since the resurrection body implies the presence of the spirit to which it belongs, whatever had made it impossible for the disembodied spirits of the Old Testament saints to leave Hades and receive their glorified resurrection bodies, that too, by virtue of those opened graves, was now removed.

Thus, the opening of Hades was the counterpart to the opening of the graves. That is, the entire nature of death, the spirit's separation from the body as well as the body's natural decay, was now virtually abolished for the saints.

Every saint in Hades could then be removed from Hades and be reunited to their bodies, now glorified and incorruptible. There was no longer any obstacle preventing it, and it was now only a question of God's appointed time.

Saints Not Now in Hades

And in light of the victory that was accomplished, God's saints will no longer enter Hades, that place where God once comforted His Old Testament saints, though their freedom was restricted. Ever since the resurrection and ascension of Christ, they have ascended to Him, far above all heavens.

Not only that, but Jesus brought back with Him all those Old Testament saints who had gone into Hades, when He Himself returned from there, and carried them with Him into heaven. The gates of Hades did not prevail against His church.

How beautifully symbolic, then, that it was by the earthquake that the graves were opened! In other words, the victory of the Savior's death had reached into "the heart of the earth" (Matthew 12:40) and had demolished the gates that had barred their passage.

That victory in "the heart of the earth" reverberated to the surface. The trembling earth and splitting rocks were symbols of the joyful revolution that had been accomplished for the Old Testament saints in Hades.

What Saints are Waiting For

We can see, therefore, that a part of what was accomplished for the spirit, symbolized by the opening of the graves, has already become the blessed experience of those who have died in Christ.

Meanwhile, that which was done for the body, likewise symbolized by the opening of the graves, all saints are still waiting for. It was accomplished and is as real as though it were now true.

Every obstacle to the full and blessed resurrection of the soul and the full resurrection glory of the body was violently removed, and we believers wait only for our divine appointment to be revealed in glory.

It was the death of Jesus Christ that accomplished such a wonderful victory for us. This is the further lesson of our subject.

When were the graves opened? Precisely at the instant of His death. That instant is emphasized because the dead bodies weren't revived to life until Christ arose on the third day. The graves were opened, even though the actual coming to life was not going to take place yet. This signified that there was a direct connection between the death of Christ and the opening of the graves.

Christ Destroyed the Power of Death

Christ's death opened the graves. That is, His death destroyed the power of death. The power of death is sin. Death entered into the world by sin and is the penalty of sin. Therefore, the death of Christ, who was sinless, enabled Him to bear the penalty of sin for His people.

But death mainly consists in the separation of the soul from the life of God, the decomposition of the body illustrating merely the shadow of death.

Therefore, when Jesus died and bore the penalty of sin for His people, His death was not only in His body but much more terrifyingly in the awful affliction of His soul. He was cursed for our sake that we might be saved from the curse. In this way He extinguished the penalty of sin for us and made it possible for us to escape all the condemnation of our sin.

This was, therefore, the symbolic purpose behind the opening of the graves at the instant of His death. The power of sin to bring death was broken by His death, and all obstacles to our attaining true eternal life, both of soul and body, were entirely removed.

The Truth of Atonement

Here the truth of the atonement is taught, the fact that God's justice was satisfied by the means of the suffering and death of our gracious Substitute.

Unless that which was symbolized by the opening of the graves had really taken place, Christ Himself could not have risen. He came to remove the obstacles to our attaining eternal life. In order to do that, He had to take upon Himself the very curse of God upon sin. If, therefore, He had not extinguished the curse, and thus made it possible to remove from us the condemnation of sin, the curse of sin would have remained on Him, and He would not have been able to escape death Himself.

If that were true, then there would have been no external evidence of His accomplishment, no removing of obstacles, no victory at all if He had not risen.

It is impossible, therefore, that the symbolism should have been any different than it was. Those dead bodies could not have been revived until the victory on our behalf had been pronounced. But that victory, proclaimed in the resurrection of Christ, was the reward of His death.

The Prison Doors Opened

Jesus' death opened those prison doors, removed the guard, and cleared the way. His own resurrection was the first use of that new freedom.

His death guaranteed for His people the blessings of their resurrection in that it abolished the obstacles to that new life. His resurrection was the imparting of that blessedness upon His people.

His death allowed us to be legally freed from the penalty of sin; His resurrection is the actual deliverance itself.

His death allowed us to be pardoned from sin; His resurrection is the proof that the payment was accepted.

His death opened Hades; His resurrection emptied Hades. His death is the grave opened, His resurrection is the dead bodies of His saints rising from their graves into life incorruptible and eternal!

Salvation Offered Today

Such is the redeeming power of the death of Jesus Christ. "The tombs broke open" (Matthew 27:52). As a result, there no longer remain any obstacles to anyone being personally delivered from eternal death. "Whoever hears My word and believes Him who sent me," Jesus said, "has crossed over from death to life" (John 5:24), and "will never die" (John 11:26).

All who place their trust in Christ have been freed in their conscience from the condemnation of sin and live now as children of God, because they have already passed from death into life.

In the meantime, their mortal bodies wait for their divine appointment, because all obstructions have been removed. The path from the grave up to the very presence of God, where nothing but eternal joy and pleasure await them, has been cleared.

The Work Is Finished

At the instant of Christ's death the graves were opened. Remember that. At the very instant of His death all our sins were completely answered for. The graves were not just partly opened; the obstacles were not just partly removed.

There is nothing left for us to achieve in regard to our pardon and acceptance with God. We are able to add nothing to the work of Christ. Our salvation from sin is in Him at this very moment, and it is perfect. What you and I need to do is receive Him and enjoy Him. Remember, "Whoever does not believe will be condemned" (Mark 16:16).

> Just as I am, without one plea
> But that Thy blood was shed for me,
> And that Thou bid'st me come to Thee,
> O Lamb of God, I come.

5

THE UNDISTURBED GRAVE CLOTHES OF CHRIST

Simon Peter, who was behind him, arrived and went into the tomb. He saw the strips of linen lying there, as well as the burial cloth that had been around Jesus' head. The cloth was folded up by itself, separate from the linen. Finally the other disciple, who had reached the tomb first, also went inside. He saw and believed. (John 20:6–8)

THE FIFTH MIRACLE OF CALVARY WAS THE REMARK-
able arrangement of things in the grave of
the recently risen Christ. The purpose of this text
is not simply to affirm the fact of the Resurrection, but to visually display it in the process.
From this perspective it ranks with the other Calvary miracles, which outwardly testified to the
value and effectiveness of His redeeming death.

Why Matthew's Omission?

It is interesting that Matthew, whose account of
the Calvary miracles is otherwise complete, makes
no reference to the circumstances before us. The
explanation of that omission is interesting. What
strikes us in Matthew's account is that it is consecutive. After mentioning the darkness—the sign
of the sufferings of the cross—he mentions the
signs of the victory of the cross, beginning with
the second of the two loud cries from the cross,
and limiting his remarks to the effects of that victory cry. It tore the curtain of the temple, shook

the earth, and opened the graves. And, in explanation of the opened graves, Matthew states that many bodies of dead saints arose from their graves after the Lord Himself had risen.

Evidently, in so perfectly consecutive a statement, there was no room between the opening of the graves and the resurrections of the saints for a description of the state of affairs in the deserted tomb of Jesus.

Matthew does mention the Lord's resurrection as the forerunner and cause of that which occurred to the saints. But it did not harmonize with his arrangement to insert an account of the condition of the tomb, because that condition was not brought about as a result of the victory cry uttered days before.

After mentioning the first four of the Calvary miracles, Matthew then goes on to describe the rising of the saints, the sixth and last wonder, but omits this fifth miracle.

An Approach to a Description of the Resurrection

However, what Matthew leaves out, John supplies. John, while mentioning none of the other Calvary miracles, nonetheless provides the best description of the Lord's resurrection, making it possible for us to consider a number of its various aspects.

Very early on Sunday morning, Peter and John heard from Mary Magdalene that the body of Jesus, placed in the tomb on Friday afternoon, was no longer there. She also announced her opinion that enemies had removed it.

Instantly the two apostles hurried to the tomb, John outrunning Peter and arriving first. He "bent over and looked in at the strips of linen lying there but did not go in" (John 20:5). But Peter, "who was behind him, arrived and went into the tomb. He saw the strips of linen lying there, as well as the burial cloth that had been around Jesus' head. The cloth was folded up by itself, separate from the linen" (John 20:6–7). After this John also went in and "He saw and believed" (John 20:8).

When Peter and John entered the tomb they did not see the body of Jesus, but they did see the grave clothes. Furthermore, they saw the clothes in a certain order—"the linen lying there," and the burial cloth that had been around Jesus head was "folded up by itself, separate from the linen."

That this was intended to describe a wonderful state of affairs is evident from the fact that it is the main subject of one whole Scripture narrative. The sole purpose of these nine verses of gospel history is to acquaint us with the exact arrangement of the grave clothes of Jesus. Obviously, spending such a large amount of time on this specific issue emphasizes its extreme importance.

The Impression of John

Correspondingly, look closely at the impression this scene made on the mind of John. He "saw and believed."

Believed what—Mary Magdalene's story that the body wasn't there? As you can see, when he saw for himself that it wasn't there it would hardly be necessary to add that he also didn't think it was there. Besides, what did the arrangement of the grave clothes have to do with his seeing that the body was not there? Yet it was precisely seeing that arrangement that caused him to believe.

Or did the statement "he saw and believed" simply mean that he believed Mary's statement that since the body wasn't there, the enemies of

Jesus had stolen it? No, because that is what the precise arrangement of clothes firmly contradicted. It is inconceivable that if someone had indeed stolen the body they would have taken the time to remove it from the clothes and then neatly arrange them. And why is John's response so different from Peter in regard to believing? Not only is nothing said of Peter's believing, but, as Luke shares with us, upon seeing "the strips of linen lying by themselves," Peter merely went away "wondering to himself what had happened" (Luke 24:12), whereas John believed at once.

Comparing John with Peter

Does this story merely mean that Peter was having trouble believing that the body had been stolen, while John was more gullible? Was John simply more naive than Peter? No, there is only one possible meaning here. When John saw the arrangement of the grave clothes, he instantly believed that Jesus had risen. The arrangement of the clothes so clearly expressed a divine intervention that he became instantly convinced of the Lord's resurrection, even though, as is added in the next verse, he had yet to understand from the Scriptures that Jesus had to rise from the dead (John 20:9).

The specific arrangement of the grave clothes was designed to produce just such an effect and visually portray the Resurrection. In that vein, let us proceed to interpret the text.

He saw "the strips of linen lying there," that is, not simply lying on the floor of the tomb, but lying there precisely where His body had been laid. They remained in exactly the position His body had occupied. Furthermore, the burial cloth that had been around Jesus' head was "by itself," not mingled with the body clothes but on the very spot where His head had rested.

It was also "folded up." In other words, when Jesus' head was removed it caused the clothes to collapse upon themselves and shrink. They had not been manually unfolded, and none of the fastenings were undone, indicating that it had not been removed from the head, but that the head had been removed from it. And there they lay, the linen clothes, the cloth for His head, nothing undone, none of the folds disturbed, no change in their position. They had simply collapsed.

Luke's Corroborative Testimony

This is the essence of what these words are describing, and in fact, they are the required understanding in order to comprehend the effect the scene had on John. Indeed, it is what Luke is attempting to express in this one phrase. And while he makes no reference to the burial cloth which had been around Jesus' head, he says that the linen clothes were "lying by themselves" (Luke 24:12).

But what is the phrase "lying by themselves" referring to? Obviously, the body itself. While the body was missing, the clothes were lying in such a way as to suggest the body. The inference here is that were the grave clothes still containing the body of Christ, they would be lying in precisely the position they were presently in. In that sense they were lying "by themselves."

The Natural Body Dissolved

The natural body had dissolved within its wrappings and merged with the spiritual body in a transformation that no burial cloth fasteners could prevent, and with such buoyancy of life that it could no longer linger amid the physical trappings of death. It vanished from within the grave clothes, moving through the great rock seal at the door of the tomb (which had not yet been removed).

Blossoming from the dead seed buried beneath the ground, disappearing without disturbing the knots and foldings, His body sprouted forth, through the massive stone, into the glorious flower of resurrection!

That is the incredible picture of resurrection left behind by the grave clothes of the risen Jesus, even though it is not a description of the act of resurrection itself. It is amazing that, while the fact of the Lord's resurrection is proclaimed in Scripture everywhere, the act itself is never described. We do not hear so much, "Then He arose and left the tomb," but "He has risen" (Matthew 28:7).

This is an example of how the writers restrained their imaginations, an experience almost as wonderful as the event itself—an internal proof of the truth of the history, which cannot be explained apart from the divine inspiration of the Scriptures.

It should come as no surprise, therefore, that having before him such a glorious display of the process of resurrection, John's keen perceptions would cause him to believe. It was a wonder designed to convince, a miraculous demonstration.

If the friends of Jesus had taken Him away they would not have removed the clothes from His body; if enemies took the body, they would not have left the clothes so neatly arranged as to invite a misunderstanding. In fact, there is no way anyone could have removed the body from its burial clothes without leaving traces of having disturbed both the linens and the burial cloth that had been about His head.

The Presence of God

It was God who had been there. Those silent memorials, those shriveled clothes lying so undisturbed, as though they still sought vainly to clutch the vanished body—the condition of things was as much a testimony to the presence and power of God as are the dry shores of a pond whose waters have evaporated and floated invisibly upward to form clouds. Except, in this case, it was a result of the presence of God's miraculous power.

A Perfect Demonstration

And this demonstration was perfect in all of its parts.

First, John personally knew that Jesus had really died and been buried. But seeing the clothes that had been on Jesus' body reminded him of it.

Secondly, it was clear that the body was missing from the tomb on the third morning, he could see that with his own eyes, for the empty grave clothes were lying by themselves.

And thirdly, by looking at the miraculous arrangement of the grave clothes he could clearly tell that the body had not been removed by human intervention. The sequential progress of events in Christ's resurrection was revealed to the eyes of John in that small tomb the moment his eyes fixed on the scene.

The Historical Argument

Now notice a remarkable thing. The historical argument for the Lord's resurrection perfectly conforms to the visual evidence that confronted John.

What is the historical argument? First, to the fact that Jesus had really died and been buried, the Jews, Romans, and disciples all equally agreed. Secondly, that on the third morning His body was missing from the tomb they all agreed. Thirdly, that His disciples didn't remove it was obvious to all, since it was physically impossible for them to have overpowered the Roman guard. These are three strong historical points.

However, there are other arguments that confirm the truth of the Resurrection, such as the personal appearances of Jesus after His resurrection and the moral power of the truth of His resurrection as evidenced in the hearts and lives of Christians. These arguments, however, were still future at the time of His resurrection, and would have no effect on an unbeliever. But the three historical points mentioned above were obvious even then to every thinker and have always been the fundamental historical argument. They possess, in themselves, an argument so powerful that few facts in history can compare to them.

God's Model of an Argument

These are the exact three points that satisfied John as he gazed into the tomb. They were, however, presented to John *inside* the tomb, where as they are presented to us *outside* the tomb.

So that scene in the tomb was God's own example of an argument for the Savior's resurrection. As we see how the historical arguments outside the tomb conform to the divine example inside the tomb, we can't help but be impressed with this spectacular evidence of God's sovereignty. In their corroborative testimonies we triumph in our living Christ.

But now look at what else is taught in that marvelous scene.

First, that it was a Calvary miracle is immediately apparent. What other death in human history has ever had such a following? Didn't Jesus say that He came to "give His life as a ransom for many" (Matthew 20:28)? By virtue of those grave clothes, clearly expressing His resurrection, the sacrifice of His life became an effective ransom.

Didn't He say that His blood would be "poured out for many for the forgiveness of sins" (Matthew 26:28)? By virtue of these empty grave clothes, the pouring out of His blood obtained the forgiveness of sins.

Did He come to be made a curse for us? By virtue of these grave clothes the curse that caused

God to abandon His Son, displayed so vividly in the darkness at noon, rolled away the curse from all those who are His.

Did He come to deliver us from every disability and introduce us to the perfect blessedness of resurrection? By virtue of those grave clothes Jesus became the first example of accomplished deliverance from sin and death and the model and prototype of the risen man.

So for all His children, Christ's death at Calvary was the destruction of death itself; because His death was sufficient, He Himself was able to rise.

The Natural Body and the Spiritual Body

Secondly, the body that lay in the grave was the foundation of His resurrection body. The disappearance of that body is set forth here as synonymous with His resurrection. His body wasn't there, and immediately John believed He had risen. While the body disappeared, the clothes remained behind, in this way identifying His buried body as that which had comprised His risen body.

As a result, it is not true, as some say, that the resurrected bodies of Christians are separated from their mortal bodies upon their death. The Scriptures teach that the resurrection of Christ is the model for our own. The spiritual and incorruptible body will be produced from the natural and corruptible body of every Christian, dead or alive, at a future time.

And since Christ's resurrection body is the model of what ours is to be, then however our bodies may be decomposed and scattered, by virtue of those grave clothes, the mysterious nature of our bodies is pronounced imperishable, singularly indestructible.

The Nature of the Resurrection Body

And yet this is not to imply that the same exact particles must reappear in the resurrection body any more than the buried seed, by which Paul illustrates this subject, is reproduced in just the same exact particles in the plant which grows from it. Yet, the buried seed is the foundation and origin of the plant, passing its own identity into the plant, and out of its own ugliness and decay, there springs forth the amazing stalk, leaf, flower, and fruit.

Thirdly, the resurrection body, while still a genuine body, is not a fleshly body as we're used to, but a spiritual body. It is a real material body, but conformed to the spirit. In other words, it has not turned into spirit, but has been designed, refined, and modified to become in all ways the perfect companion to the human spirit.

Comparing Jesus' Resurrection to that of Lazarus

This truth is illustrated in the disappearance of Jesus' body from His grave clothes. While Jesus left behind His grave clothes, Lazarus came forth, "his hands and feet wrapped with strips of linen, and a cloth around his face" (John 11:44).

Notice the corresponding difference. Lazarus returned to the same life as before; Jesus did not. Lazarus came back to his fleshly body with the same weaknesses and sicknesses as before; Jesus did not. Lazarus died again, and even now waits for "a better resurrection" (Hebrews 11:35), while Jesus can never die again. What symbolical relics, then, were those empty grave clothes in the Lord's tomb!

That the Lord had all the weaknesses of human flesh (although without sin) before He died and rose again, we know, but He never had any weaknesses afterward. He was once a weary traveler, His feet sore and Himself exhausted. After He was risen, He was talking with the two disciples from Emmaus. When their eyes were opened to recognize Him, He vanished out of their sight, precisely as He had eluded the fastenings of His grave clothes without undoing them.

Therefore, a true resurrection is very different from a mere revival from the dead. Lazarus, though in one sense risen from the dead, was still a mortal man among other mortals.

The true resurrection body, while still a genuine body, is not simply a fleshly body, but a body according to the spirit. When Jesus Christ left His grave clothes behind, it was symbolic of the fact that He had gotten rid of the flesh as flesh, that is, of the weakness and physical consistency characteristic of all those who are born into this world. And when He left His grave clothes, emptying them of Himself by vanishing from within them, it demonstrated that He had attained to a spiritual body condition. This condition is independent of the laws of physics, with powers similar to the wind, making it impossible to tell where it comes from or where it is going. This is a condition of the incorruptible body, as swift as light, never tiring, grand, glorious.

Christ's Glory—the Believer's Glory

In this way the resurrection of Jesus Christ was the perfection, the culmination of His incarnation. At that time He became man as He will forever remain—not in the "likeness of sinful man" (Romans 8:3), in which condition He was merely a sojourner, but in a renovated humanity and in the "power of an indestructible life" (Hebrews 7:16). Similarly, the people of God are destined to enter into that same condition of body and unchangeable glory; for He is the Head, they are the members. Even now their life is hid with Christ in God (Colossians 3:3). Their citizenship is in heaven. The apostle said, they "eagerly await a Savior from there, the Lord Jesus Christ, who, by the power that enables Him to bring everything under His control, will transform our lowly bodies so that they will be like His glorious body" (Philippians 3:20–21).

What a delightful hope the believer in Christ can rejoice in!

The False Pride of Men

Because of this blessed hope, how deceiving is the pride and self-sufficiency of men! They speak of progress and improvement, of individual and social advancement. From a specifically human point of view this is not to be criticized, yet these are nothing more than adjustments to the same deteriorating condition. We will never overcome the weaknesses and problems of this mortal life, so there can never be any radically satisfying improvement in our condition. We are perfected only in Christ. It will not be until that great city of God is finally revealed, whose gorgeous vision closes the Word of God, that man's dream of perfection will ever be realized.

On the jasper threshold standing,
Like a pilgrim safely landing,
See, the strange, bright scene expanding;
Ah, 'tis heaven at last!
What a city! What a glory!
Far beyond the brightest story
Of the ages old and hoary;
Ah, 'tis heaven at last!
Christ Himself the living splendor,
Christ the sunlight, mild and tender;
Praises to the Lamb we render;
Ah, 'tis heaven at last!

6

REVIVALS TO LIFE IN THE CALVARY GRAVEYARD

The tombs broke open and the bodies of many holy people who had died were raised to life. They came out of the tombs, and after Jesus' resurrection they went into the holy city and appeared to many people. (Matthew 27:52–53)

THE SIXTH MIRACLE OF CALVARY WAS THE REVIVALS to life that accompanied the resurrection of Jesus Christ.

The text reveals to us that certain graves were opened by the earthquake at the death of Christ, and that the dead bodies arose and came out of them after Christ Himself had risen, and that they went into Jerusalem and appeared to many. It is a statement of one of the grandest miracles, an incredible example of supernaturalism, supernatural in the sense that it was completely miraculous.

Let us review the historical truth of this statement. If anyone questions its historical character, it can be answered that it is as historical as anything in Scripture. Scholars universally acknowledge, in some cases reluctantly, that these words are *not* a later insertion, but a part of the genuine words of the Bible. And if there is in the entire world a document more absolutely historical than the Bible, it has yet to be discovered.

Is It an Invention?

But couldn't the evangelist have drawn on his imagination, creating from the mere fact of dead bodies exposed in graves a myth of resurrection from the dead? No. If the Bible is solemn truth from the Holy Spirit, the writer is prevented from inventing his facts to gratify an appetite for the miraculous.

"But," some will say, "it is difficult to account for such an experience, and the words are obscure." This is not true. The statement that the bodies arose and went into Jerusalem is not obscure. These words are self-evident and their meaning as visible as light. We are not concerned with accounting for the difficulty of the statement, except to consider it as divinely designed to be closely related with the death and resurrection of our Lord and Savior.

Self-Evidencing Marks

To this statement belong certain historical marks of its own. Not only is it a part of Scripture, but it is so intertwined with Scripture that it can't help but be there. It stands in the same line as the other miraculous events of the time. It harmonizes with and explains the wonder of the opened graves, in the same way that that the opened graves were the product of the miraculous earthquake. And the earthquake was the miraculous counterpart to the tearing of the curtain, and the curtain was the answer to the shout of victory from the cross whose dying Sufferer had just emerged triumphant from the horrors of the symbolic darkness! So if all the previous miracles of Calvary were historical, then in order to maintain their harmony, this is the only conceivable way the great series of miracles could end.

Moreover, it is in complete accord with the whole teaching of salvation. If we believe fully in Jesus and do not waver in disbelief at the power of His salvation, we will understand this. Instead of being amazed that the resurrection was accentuated by such revivals to life in the Calvary graveyard, we would say instead, upon hearing of the incident, that, "It has a right to be here. It is credible because it expresses the pledge of the coming resurrection, when, from all the graveyards of the world, wherever the mortal remains of a saint may lie, this corruptible shall put on incorruption, and this mortal immortality!"

Marvelous Reticence

Then again, consider the reticence of this statement. In that restraint we see a sign of truthfulness, where incredulous babbling is forced into silence, and even the severest criticism must express admiration. The evangelist tells his story of wonder; but we also have a curious story to tell on him, one barely less wonderful than his own. Our story is that these few words are absolutely all he says.

He tells us that when the Lord was resurrected certain of the departed saints arose, left their graves, and went into Jerusalem, appearing to many. But he says nothing more. Who were they? How many were there? Did they go into the houses of the people or only walk the streets? Whether they appeared only once, or from time to time during the forty days of the Lord's appearances, isn't told us. How did their return from the dead affect them? Did they speak of the realms of the dead or of Christ's recent entrance into those realms? How and when did they finally disappear, or did they continue to live? On all these questions there is not a word, not so much as the faintest recognition of the possibility of such questions being asked!

Nor does the writer even mention whether the risen saints had died recently. At first glance, it might be inferred that this is implied in their appearing to many, for why should they appear, except to be recognized and identified? And yet, Moses and Elijah were recognized by the disciples at the Transfiguration, although they had never before seen either one. Certainly the Holy Spirit is able to make known to people those who were strangers before. He is able to do it as easily and quietly as the light shines or a new idea comes into the mind.

In fact, the thought in this text is not simply that they "appeared"—which doesn't fully express the original—but that they were plainly recognized. It is not said that they were recognized by their names. The only thing implied is that they were plainly recognized as people risen from the dead.

Now how do we respond to such restraint? Was there ever a myth in any fiction story that had such a brief setting? If history can be judged by the manner in which she chronicles events, then this is history. Furthermore, it is a divine history, for what uninspired historian ever practiced such a repressed imagination? The desire to pry into the secrets of the other world can be unbearable. One of the oldest superstitions is that of trying to speak to the dead. It was forbidden in the Law of Moses. It was one of the world's mischievous pursuits in the ignorance of earlier centuries. And yet we see a revival of it even now in our intellectual age, when human beings think they have finally gained a mature knowledge of life.

So, I say, the silence in our text is almost as wonderful as the miracle itself. No one, writing about a miracle of such magnitude, would have said so little.

In the second place, what was the nature of their revivals from the dead? There are two kinds exhibited in Scripture. We are told of six resurrections that were only restorations to this present mortal life. The son of the widow of Zarephath (1 Kings 17), the Shunammite's son (2 Kings 4), the resurrection caused by the bones of Elisha (2 Kings 13), the daughter of Jairus (Matthew 9), the son of the widow of Nain (Luke 7), and Lazarus (John 11). In every one of those cases, it was only a revival of the natural body that would die again, and which, in those particular cases, undeniably did die again.

The Resurrection Proper

On the other hand, there is 1 Corinthians 15, where a resurrection body of an entirely different kind is promised to us who have placed our hope in the day of the Lord's coming. "It is sown in dishonor, it is raised in glory; it is sown in weakness, it is raised in power, it is sown a natural body, it is raised a spiritual body." (1 Corinthians 15:43–44). That is the actual resurrection—the true rising from the dead.

But in which of these two categories should we place these resurrections? Were those bodies examples of the resurrection body described in 1 Corinthians 15—spiritual, incorruptible, and immortal? Or were they only the natural body restored to this present life, like Lazarus and the others we referred to? Does the Scripture provide the means for us to answer this question?

Now in 1 Corinthians 15 we are told that *all* who are Christ's shall be made alive in the resurrection body described there. However, we read, "But each in his own turn" (1 Corinthians 15:23), each one of the "all" who will be made alive will be made alive in his own order.

And what is that order? "Christ, the first-fruits; then, when He comes, those who belong to Him" (1 Corinthians 15:23). Christ will rise first, and He did rise in that kind of final resurrected body—then afterward, at His coming, every one of the "all" who are His will be raised in that same way.

Note it well. The apostle doesn't say that only those who haven't risen before will rise at Christ's coming. His language is absolute and all-inclusive—"those who belong to Him"—he says, without making any exceptions. All those who belong to Christ shall rise, every one who is His throughout the ages. Then he adds, "but each,"—every last one—"in his own turn," and their turn he explains as being "Christ, the first-fruits," and then only "when He comes."

Notice how careful he is to tell them that this order affects all, throughout all the ages, who were ever meant to take part in that kind of resurrection.

Therefore, it is clear that none of Christ's people have yet received the spiritual immortal body, and none shall receive it until His coming. Those saints at Calvary rose from their graves, but only in their natural revived bodies. They are still waiting for their true resurrection bodies until that moment when we are all raised up to

Christ, from all the ages. No one shall precede another, no one will be perfected before another. God has provided something better for us, so that those saints who were raised at Calvary will not be made perfect without us.

But What about Enoch and Elijah?

Enoch and Elijah were taken from this life so that they did not experience death (Hebrews 11:5; 2 Kings 2:11). Didn't they have incorruptible and immortal bodies? Paul must answer the question. If Enoch and Elijah, upon being taken from this life, received the spiritual resurrection body, then Christ Himself was not the firstfruits, nor is it true that everyone who belongs to Christ through all the ages is going to be made alive exclusively at His coming.

It is not a problem that Elijah was seen in glory when he talked with Jesus on the Mount of Transfiguration, for God may illumine even our natural body with glory. Didn't Moses reflect a glory when he came down from Mount Sinai? Didn't Stephen's face appear to everyone who beheld him before his martyrdom as an angel? And didn't even the natural body of the Son of Man become as bright as the sun? And even when

He descended from the Transfiguration—when His face was still retaining that glory—weren't all the people greatly amazed when they saw Him?

Will They Return?

Therefore, let us be satisfied with the answer of Paul. Enoch and Elijah may now be in a certain kind of glory, although not their final resurrected glory. They still live in their natural bodies, for despite the corruption inherent in it, Methuselah himself lived almost one thousand years on earth. Nor is it necessary that they ever die, any more than the saints who are alive on the earth at His coming and who shall be changed and caught up together with the Lord in the air.

It is quite possible that God may one day send Enoch and Elijah back to the earth on some service, the culmination of which may result in their suffering and death. Regarding Elijah, at least, the hints of that are strong and numerous in Scripture. In any case, regarding the true resurrection body, Enoch and Elijah must also wait with us, and we shall all be made perfect together at the same moment.

It is possible that the risen saints of our story were afterward taken from this life like Enoch and Elijah, in their natural bodies, not to die again. With Elijah and Enoch, they may be now awaiting the future resurrection. This notion may be true or false. There is no authority for explicitly saying that this is true, but this we do say, they did not have then, and they do not have now, the resurrection body of 1 Corinthians 15. And since this is true, we need to recognize how essential this is to our instruction in the truth of God.

Then, in the third place, what is it that God is teaching us here? Our answer is that He is teaching us the truth and certainty of the final resurrection. The teaching is symbolical. The revivals to life of the saints at Calvary foretell the greater coming glory. They were not *the* resurrection, but they were *a* resurrection, not the thing itself, but the shadow of it. Yet they were a substantial shadow, requiring nothing less than omnipotence. This was the greater meaning behind the revivals: they were a rehearsal of the more glorious scene to come.

God has assured us numerous times of that coming resurrection glory, but here He demonstrated it for us. When Christ was finished with His work and His time had come to leave the world, the great final resurrection was hinted at on a small scale, with an expenditure of power sufficient for us to trust what He can accomplish in the future. It was a farewell display of His purpose and power, a pledge and guarantee of the Savior's return to be glorified in His risen saints.

God's Purpose in the Event

We can't know what other purposes God may have designed for them. At the least it was for this. When Jesus said, "I am the resurrection and the life" (John 11:25), and proved this truth by raising Lazarus from the dead, the proof didn't lie in what kind of body Lazarus was raised with. Chapter 15 of 1 Corinthians demonstrates the meaning of Jesus being the resurrection and the life. But the proof lay in the fact that restoring Lazarus to natural life, the shadow of the true resurrection, still required and visibly displayed the omnipotent power necessary for both resurrections.

Indeed, combining both the historic with the symbolic is a significant feature of the entire series of Calvary miracles. The three hours of darkness, though real, was merely a symbol. The tearing of the curtain as though an artisan's blade had cut it from top to bottom was a symbol. The earthquake that split the rocks was a symbol. The opened graves were a symbol. The grave clothes of Jesus, whose marvelous arrangement was a demonstration to John of his Lord's resurrection, were a symbol. And here, these revivals from the dead, living realities yet still only symbolic, completed the harmonious arrangement of miracles.

A Ground of Assurance

With that powerful scene in mind, how forcefully vivid does our assurance in the final resurrection become! When an event that has actually occurred is understood to be representative, its symbolism becomes more than just a verbal expression of ideas but an acting out of them as well.

One of the most beautiful things Jesus ever said was "I am the vine; you are the branches" (John 15:5). Were an artist to paint a picture of vine and branches on his canvas, you would have a picture of the essential union of Christ and believers, but still only a picture. But let us say, for example, that you were looking at a particular grapevine and while doing so came to understand that God planted it for the specific purpose of serving as an analogy to you of your union with Him. Think of how much more impressive your sense of the union between Christ and believers would become!

Symbols and Analogies

In the same way, the white robes seen on the multitude in the book of Revelation, while a symbol of their final resurrection glory, were only a picture, for they did not yet actually exist. But the situations in the Calvary graveyard were actual instances of death destroyed for a specific time and natural life restored in the grave—instances of God's omnipotence working amid human decay and producing restoration. Those revived bodies of saints walking the streets of Jerusalem were designed by God as a representation, a foreshadowing of immortality and eternal glory; but as actual occurrences they also demonstrated the certainty of that which they represented.

Grandeur of the Plan

Furthermore, what an amazing impression is made upon us of the grandeur of God's plan! When we consider that those saints did not have the body that was "sown in weakness" and "raised in power" (1 Corinthians 15:43), God's purpose in making the final resurrection a beautiful expression of the unity of the Body of Christ, the church, is clarified.

"Those who belong to Him" (1 Corinthians 15:23). No member of the Body will be glorified before another. Its eye, its hand, its foot, its greatest and its least, whether the remains be under the snows of Greenland or the burning soil of Africa, they shall together be ushered into the fullness of eternal life. At that time the whole Body, drawn from throughout the ages, shall come forth at exactly the same moment in a perfect harmony of beauty and glory.

Another lesson is that only in the personal deliverance of Christ Himself are His people delivered. The saints of Calvary rose from the dead only after and because Christ Himself rose from the dead. "They came out of the tombs, and after Jesus' resurrection they went into the Holy City" (Matthew 27:53).

While it is true that their revival was not their final resurrection and their restored bodies were not yet created like His glorious resurrection body, yet they still lived in their restored bodies, the magnificent symbol of the final resurrection.

Now, being such a symbol, they are immediately and deliberately placed in view following

Christ's resurrection. They went forth from their graves, so to speak, on the very heels of Jesus. They followed Him as meaning follows language, as vision follows light.

Jesus First

In other words, only by extinguishing the curse of sin and conquering it in His own person has Jesus Christ succeeded in removing it from His people.

Since He was the One designated to bear the sins for us all, had He not personally been declared righteous before the Father through the accepted offering of His perfect sufferings, we could have never been justified by faith. Had He not achieved true resurrection Himself, neither would we have been able to. Consequently, His people are in Him and are one with Him. His death was their death; His life is their life. "Because I live, you also will live," He said (John 14:19).

Oh, the immeasurable assurance of our promised heritage! We are joined with Christ in the same bundle of life. Even now "your life is now hidden with Christ in God" (Colossians 3:3) and a time is coming when "[He] will transform our lowly bodies so that they will be like His glorious body" (Philippians 3:21).

And keep one more thing in mind. Only those who are Christ's shall ever attain to the resurrection body of 1 Corinthians 15.

Only "saints" were revived from the dead in the graveyard of Calvary. No one, therefore, except saints shall be in that "great multitude that no one could count, from every nation, tribe, people and language, standing before the throne and in front of the Lamb. They were wearing white robes and were holding palm branches in their hands" (Revelation 7:9). Those "many" of Calvary symbolize the "great multitude" of heaven.

Those who do not belong to Christ shall rise out of their graves also, but it will not be because of the saving blood of Christ. Jesus said, "those who have done good will rise to live, and those who have done evil will rise to be condemned" (John 5:29). Instead of being resurrected from the regions of the dead, they will be plunged into "the second death" (Revelation 21:8). Only the children of God shall "rise to live" (John 5:29).

No one will rise but saints, and yet *every* saint—because everyone who believes in Jesus is a saint—and the person who believes in Him has everlasting life and shall never be condemned.

NOTE TO THE READER

The publisher invites you to share your response to the message of this book by writing Discovery House Publishers, P. O. Box 3566, Grand Rapids, MI 49501, USA or by calling 1-800-653-8333. For information about other Discovery House publications, contact us at the same address and phone number. Find us on the Internet at http://www.dhp.org/ or send e-mail to books@dhp.org.